NASCAR
Champions

KASEY KAHNE

Connor Dayton

PowerKiDS press™

New York

Published in 2008 by The Rosen Publishing Group, Inc.
29 East 21st Street, New York, NY 10010

First Edition

Editor: Jennifer Way
Book Design: Michael J. Flynn
Layout Design: Kate Laczynski
Photo Researcher: Nicole Pristash

Photo Credits: All images © Getty Images.

Library of Congress Cataloging-in-Publication Data

Dayton, Connor.
  Kasey Kahne / Connor Dayton. — 1st ed.
      p. cm. — (NASCAR champions)
  Includes index.
  ISBN-13: 978-1-4042-3815-2 (library binding)
  ISBN-10: 1-4042-3815-8 (library binding)
  1. Kahne, Kasey, 1980– 2. Stock car drivers—United States—Biography—Juvenile literature.
I. Title.
  GV1032.K34D39 2008
  796.72092—dc22
  [B]
                                    2007001983

Manufactured in the United States of America

DATE DUE

APR 01 2010		
AUG 08 2013		
AUG 01 2015		

Demco

Contents

Kasey Kahne was born on April 10, 1980, in Enumclaw, Washington. He now lives in Mooresville, North Carolina.

4

Kahne was interested in racing cars from a young age. When he turned 18, he began to race in the NASCAR Busch **Series**.

6

In 2002, Kahne signed with the Robert Yates Racing team. Each NASCAR team has drivers, cars, and a **pit crew**.

Kasey Kahne moved up to the Nextel Cup Series of races in 2004. This is the top NASCAR series.

10

Kahne did great in his first year in the Nextel Cup Series. He was named that series' 2004 **Rookie** of the Year.

12

Raybestos
The best in brakes
NASCAR
ROOKIE OF THE YEAR

2004

Kasey Kahne

13

Kahne quickly became famous with NASCAR fans. He went from being an unknown driver to a household name in under a year!

14

In the 2005 **season**, Kahne struggled to remain a top racer. Kahne **improved** in the 2006 season. That year he finished eighth overall.

16

Kasey Kahne races a Dodge Charger for the Evernham Motorsports team.

18

19

Kasey Kahne also does **charity** work. He set up the Kasey Kahne **Foundation** to give money to help sick children.

KASEY KAHNE
FOUNDATION

2005-9

_____ 20 _____

PAY TO THE ORDER OF _____ *Cornerstone Schools* _____ $ _**10,000**_

Ten Thousand and 00/100 _____ DOLLARS

Kasey Kahne **21**

Glossary

charity (CHER-uh-tee) A group that gives help to the needy.

foundation (fown-DAY-shun) A group set up to give help for a cause.

improved (im-PROOVD) Got better.

pit crew (PIT KROO) The people on a racing team who work on the cars.

rookie (RU-kee) A new player or driver.

season (SEEZ-un) The group of games or races for a year.

series (SIR-eez) A group of races.

Books and Web Sites

Books

Buckley, James. *NASCAR (DK Eyewitness Books)*. New York: DK Books, 2005.

Kelley, K.C. *NASCAR Daring Drivers*. Pleasantville, NY: Reader's Digest Books, 2005.

Web Sites

Due to the changing nature of Internet links, the Rosen Publishing Group, Inc., has developed an online list of Web sites related to the subject of this book. This site is updated regularly. Please use this link to access the list: www.powerkidslinks.com/nas/kkah/

23

Index